Harbour Doubts

Bebe Ashley lives in Northern Ireland and works at the Seamus Heaney Centre at Queen's University Belfast. Her debut collection *Gold Light Shining* (Banshee Press, 2020) was selected for the Arts Council's Read Mór programme in 2022. Her work is most recently published in *Granta, The Stinging Fly, bath magg,* and *Modern Poetry in Translation.* In 2023, Bebe received the Ivan Juritz Prize for Creative Experiment (Text) and a Creative Practitioner Bursary from Belfast City Council. In 2024, Bebe received the British Council Fellowship for Bundanon, Australia. www.bebe-ashley.com

Harbour Doubts

Bebe Ashley

First published 2025 by Banshee Press
www.bansheepress.org

Copyright © Bebe Ashley, 2025
First edition

No part of this publication may be reproduced in any form or by any means without the prior written permission of the publisher.

All rights reserved.

A CIP record for this title is available from the British Library.

Grateful acknowledgement is made to Granta Books for permission to reproduce material from *Scattered All Over the Earth* by Yoko Tawada © 2022 Granta Books; *The Last Children of Tokyo* by Yoko Tawada © 2018 Granta Books; and *Memoirs of a Polar Bear* by Yoko Tawada © 2017 Granta Books

Banshee Press gratefully acknowledges
the financial assistance of the Arts Council.

ISBN: 978-1-917161-00-8

Set in Palatino by Eimear Ryan
Cover design by Jack Smyth
Printed in Ireland by Walsh Colour Print

Dedication TK

Contents

[have]	3
Sue Thomas F.B.Eye	5
Instruction Manual I: COMMUNITY	7
Conversation Skills	8
Sign Language Linguistics	9
I Watch the Interpreter Closely	10
First Mistake	11
Dinner Party	12
Most Recent Mistake (Now, I'll translate…)	13
Instruction Manual II: LET'S SIGN	14
Let's Sign Science	15
Let's Sign Minibeasts	16
Instruction Manual III: DISTRACTION	17
Writing Audio Description at the Ulster Museum	18
The Lookout	19
Tom Daley Dives for David Hockney / David Hockney Paints Tom Daley	20
Instruction Manual IV: KINDNESS	21
The Olive Branch	22
Sappho, who is doing you wrong?	23
I hear the rocks and stones	24
[have doubts]	25
Three Summer Birthdays	27
[harbour doubts]	29
an experimental translation	31
Acknowledgements	6

Harbour Doubts

[have]

'If you get lonely, come right home' a friend told me, looking troubled just like the grownups. I had no idea what loneliness was yet so I wasn't worried.

– Yoko Tawada, *Scattered All Over the Earth*
translated by Margaret Mitsutani

Sue Thomas F.B.Eye

It started with something I saw on the television.
I was fifteen, doing homework on the leather sofa

as the pasta water boiled furiously, rolling steam
across the kitchen ceiling. There was a new, short-lived,

crime drama in English and American Sign Language
and I was beginning to fall in love with the future.

Leaving fingerprints behind, Sue gets a promotion
and moves into an apartment above a bowling alley.

Noise from its neon light doesn't bother her because
she cannot hear it and friends still visit her anyway.

I list everything Sue has and circle the things I think I need:
a salary, a golden retriever, and a slow-burn office romance.

*

I start speaking ambidextrously and learn the alphabet,
again. I twist and trace my fingers into new formations

then stretch the tight muscles at the base of my thumb.
I learn to read and write and talk to myself simultaneously.

I better understand the distance between my own body
and the space I make for meaning to form in front of me.

The things I want to say have always been there but invisible, until I make them visible in their small, confident pockets of air.

In school, I write sentences with a fountain pen
and fingerspell the language spoken underneath the desk.

Sometimes I come home hot with shame. If there is an absence
of language, I panic.
					I panic.

Instruction Manual I

It is normal to have a crisis of confidence before committing to a career path. Nobody knows how best to spend a life. An important characteristic of an interpreter is resilience. You may find exams interrupted by an incipient pandemic, mental encumbrance or something else exceptionally unforeseen. At this time, you may find comfort in reaching out to the local COMMUNITY.

Conversation Skills

I'm not always a natural conversationalist.
At parties, at pubs, I slink to the side of the room

where I'm not expected to be the life of the party
but reliable in supporting local artists, and my friends.

This morning, I've had twenty minutes to revise my opinions
on the British Sign Language (Scotland) Act 2015.

I decline to discuss d/Deaf representation in film
because I still haven't seen A Quiet Place,

I don't want to anticipate the jump scares, or to admit
that I miss the cinema and its cardboard popcorn.

I establish a backstory of not entirely improbable details:
I was unhappy at the rain this morning but am taken aback

by the now beautiful sunshine over south Belfast.
I slept well. I will have to leave early to catch a train.

Waiting to be let into the virtual examination room,
I jeopardize my phonology with honey and lavender hand cream.

Sign Language Linguistics

In my first linguistics lesson, I keep stacking
the animals on top of each other in the zoo

in the same enclosure, sharing the same
topographical signing space, the same view.

The Bengal tigers are sunning themselves
between crocodiles in the hippopotamus's pool.

The pandas are preoccupied with the peacock's plumage;
the Alpine ibex are taunting the lazy kangaroos.

Before I point to things, I have to decide
whether they really are where I say they are

so I practice with the planets, and the sun,
stupendous in the centre of the room.

I keep Mercury close to the coffee table,
let Venus and Mars watch over heirlooms,

I fling Jupiter and Saturn onto the lampshade,
let Uranus and Neptune rattle alongside bottles of perfume.

I acknowledge the empty spaces then encounter Earth,
luminous in its orbit of slight ellipticity.

I Watch the Interpreter Closely

I'm not the target demographic for a Friday night
presentation on osteo- or rheumatoid arthritis.

I'm confronted by complex spelling patterns,
by muscle memory and inflammation.

I take notes on atmospheric pressure and painkillers,
on the double movement of a magic cure.

A tilt of the head tells me the difference
between being high and being high up.

It's nearly time for the squash and biscuits.
In a still moment, I alphabetize my vocabulary.

First Mistake

SOME SIGNS
DIFFERENT HERE
I LEARNED IN BUTTER

Dinner Party

Mum thinks I'm asking for the langoustines
mais j'explique que je travaille en langue des signes.

Most Recent Mistake

(Now, I'll translate …)

I know that the sign is wrong, the moment
that I have signed it. The pages of my translation
have leapt from the safety and accuracy
of my palm to the unmothered son born
on the back of my wrist. Nobody seems to notice
I have stuttered because in a lifetime they have made
no attempt to learn the language themselves. It is
the only thing I remember of what I wanted to say.

Instruction Manual II

There are many British Sign Language books and dictionaries, of varying print quality, available to supplement in-person sign language learning. Themed vocabulary for Christmas or Halloween can have many real-life practical applications. One popular series is LET'S SIGN.

Let's Sign Science

For a visual poetry class, I am photocopying pages
from *Let's Sign Science: BSL Vocabulary*
from an old series of print publications
that also includes *Let's Sign Feelings & Emotions*.

I would like to find *Let's Sign Song Lyrics*
or *Let's Sign In the Museum* but they don't exist.
Pop culture is never a priority and I can't afford a year of
fine-line art classes to learn to draw moving hands myself.

I cut out cool collage combinations like untamed
magnetic attraction or caterpillar camouflage.
Something is missing but these are all the words I have.
I arrange the language and it falls flat on the page.

Let's Sign Minibeasts

Every morning I check the kettle for slugs.
In the downstairs hallway, on warmer mornings,
the brocade wallpaper peels from the walls.
On colder nights, it crinkles and cracks appear.
In the right light, I can sometimes see a silver trail
winding along the crevices of the knotted treads.
The kitchen tap drips when the washing machine runs.
The lino in the shower is pulled together with duct tape.
There was once a giant spider in the bathtub,
morally impossible to kill until a miscommunication
and a mixing bowl of cold water washed it right
up and over the lip of the bath and into the unknown.
I haven't seen a slug in six months but I know
they still contort themselves between the floorboards.

Instruction Manual III

A successful freelancer knows how to diversify their portfolio. A performance interpreter might also want to qualify as a speech-to-text transcriber, or write scripts for audio description. Acquiring this range of skills is called DISTRACTION.

Writing Audio Description at the Ulster Museum

I want to talk you through the time and space of early California.
The brushstrokes are confident in the white span of sea foam.
The colours are cold and I am sure the sea wall is seeping.

I am happy in the landscapes I've never seen in person.
It does not matter that this is a windowless room,
Venice Beach is well lit and I wouldn't want to change my view.

The pigment of the watercolour is easily saturated in the paper.
I am trying to list the most important blues when
I am distracted by something new: a close, but different blue.

The Lookout

It is probable that poetry is being born somewhere in the stillness of the night when the Republican soldier looks up at the stars, or hears the rabbit rustle in the fern.
— 'Saturday Review' in *The Irish Book Lover*, vol. XII

The scraps of paper shoved down the inside ankle
    of a boot are there for emergencies. It's easy to forget
yourself when the hills come & go with the cloud cover

    & the heartbreak has been relentless. By now, even you
are suspicious of the rabbit rustling through the fern
    & of the hedgehog emerging from the heliotrope.

A night with no stars is not a good night.
    You are wearing down the lead of the pencil
in your coat pocket. The paper dampens quickly

    & being no distance from the lough will help.
If you look north long enough, you'll see sparks
    from somebody else's safety matches reflected

in the gorse & you'll appreciate the risk:
    a brisk wind would carry fire across the island.

Tom Daley Dives for David Hockney
David Hockney Paints Tom Daley

after Tariq Thompson

Tom Daley is not looking down.
He counts to three. He leaps! He shrieks
in synchronized vowel sounds!

He tries not to twist past the fluorescents
more than twice but pikes and extends
towards the rushing light of blue.

Alive, he floats to the surface
with an irregular heartbeat
and his breath left underwater.

David Hockney begins towelling off.
Cellulose paper absorbs the incorrect
composition of pool chemicals and paint.

Instruction Manual IV

Until you have stood up in a room full of people sitting down, you may forget how uncomfortable you are at having people look at you for extended periods of time. Some people will adjust to this feeling with time or treat it as stage fright. Others may find this debilitating and be in need of the comfort of KINDNESS.

The Olive Branch

I am listening to a podcast where people share
their experiences of failure and thinking of you.

I still believe there is nothing more romantic
than learning a language for somebody specific
so I couldn't help but stop when you said
surely sexuality was just another language
I could gain mastery of or certificates in
& being unable to pronounce its vocabulary meant
I was fluent in a language I'd never speak aloud.

I appropriate the love stories of fictional characters.
I don't know how to write the absence of my own.

Sappho, who is doing you wrong?

A Kintsugi of Sappho

Even in another time, someone somewhere
will remember us.

Even in another time, swift sparrows
stretch over salt sea to the loveliest stars.

Even in another time, the dawn light scatters
your laughter glittering on this coal-black earth.

Even in another time, my wild soul here
like a hyacinth in the mountains.

Even in another time, I want to say something
but shame sends me stuttering.

Even in another time, Sappho,
who is doing you wrong?

Even in another time, I am weary
of your words, and your soft, strange ways.

I Hear the Rocks and Stones

The forest is dark and thick with bramble and blackthorn.
It is night. I had been walking for so long towards
a warm light which I was sure promised security,
that I stumbled and lost sight of the other life
guiding the railroad ahead of me. I am scared this is
a sabotage of my own making. They don't wait for me,
but I hear encouragement from the people I had planned
my route with. They are calling, clamouring! from the ecotone,
casting me in their lamplight. This lucidity is only momentary.
So many people have tried their best but so have I.
I turn my back on the path I thought I would take.
I mourn the big-hearted life that I felt so close to me.
I mourn it all: as Orpheus; as Eurydice.

[have doubts]

The shelf life of words is getting shorter ...

– Yoko Tawada, *The Last Children of Tokyo*
translated by Margaret Mitsutani

Three Summer Birthdays

Everything changes.
Most of us lose
something or someone.

It is hard to reconcile
the people we were
with the people we are now.

[harbour doubts]
an experimental translation

Writing an autobiography means guessing or making up everything you've forgotten.

— Yoko Tawada, *Memoirs of a Polar Bear*
translated by Susan Bernofsky

TO ASK A QUESTION I RAISE MY EYEBROWS

Anticipation is my least favourite emotion.

HELLO IS THE FIRST SIGN EVERYONE LEARNS

Even in the beginning we are trying our best to be understood. Over time we become more conversational. So many things have happened since I started writing this that I can't remember what you already know. Or what I want you to know.

The most important thing to know is that I have nearly always wanted to become a sign language interpreter. This longing has been at the periphery of everything I have done. The second most important thing to know is that it is becoming clearer this isn't going to happen.

WE FIRST SHARE OUR NAMES LETTER BY LETTER
A SIGN NAME MIGHT COME OVER TIME

Nobody calls me by the name on my birth certificate.
I stumble over the fingerspelling of it, the fluency
of the letters I don't often hear aloud.

In small groups, we take turns getting to know each other.

The house is big and empty when I am only having
conversations with myself within it. I adopt Lily and Merlin
from an animal rescue in Moira. Merlin is rarely still
and if he is he snores.

A GOOD CANDIDATE DOES NOT GET DISTRACTED BY TRYING TO COMMUNICATE TANGENTIAL IDEAS

My horoscope tells me this is the year of slow, deliberate, feelings. It is true that I craft my own horoscope using the best part of everyone else's but by doing so I am making my own destiny.

I tell my students the best place to learn a three-act structure is reflected in the occluded surface of a crystal ball
and the disposition of the heavens at any particular moment:

Lately, the only thing that keeps you going is fear.
(There's a pulsing tremble in your ribcage.)
This week, don't be afraid to organize your spice cupboard.
Even if you haven't seasoned an omelette in a long time
a fresh encounter with a stranger will bring
you some much needed ease.

**NOW AND TODAY ARE VERY SIMILAR SIGNS
YOU HAVE TO BE READY TO ENCOUNTER BOTH**

Today, my neurotransmitters are reluctant to communicate.
There is too much paperwork to do so I can't do any of it.
I walk alone through the park. I see a Dalmatian and I think:
that would look good in my living room.

IT IS IMPORTANT TO STRUCTURE A LIST WELL

These jobs are not ordered by priority, or date acquired.

My first job was in a supermarket and before that my first job was cleaning my aunt's office on the weekends and before that my first job was as a babysitter and before that my first job was delivering newspapers across the village and before that my first job was being the eldest grandchild.

After I left school, my first job was in New Zealand.
I was seventeen and on my first long-haul flight cried all the way to the layover in Los Angeles.

On my first day in Auckland, I was walking towards the Domain Wintergardens considering that the same brain system that stops physical movement may detail thought processes.

The leaves were freshly shaped and I was taking in the newness of the sky until I wasn't. I was instead becoming familiar with the firmness of asphalt and the helpfulness of strangers. The same brain system that derails thought processes may stop physical movement.
I had tripped over a speed bump and fallen heavily.

The green plastic of my wristwatch shattered with the force of impact and splintered as the capillaries under my skin burst open and tender. My one pair of jeans shredded at the knees. I walked around the museum then back to my hotel to unpack my first aid kit. I was lucky to have avoided using my health insurance. I was lucky to have health insurance.

THE GOVERNMENT WAS TAKEN TO COURT THIS YEAR BECAUSE THEIR ACCESS TO INFORMATION WAS NOT EQUAL

It was literally a matter of life or death.
I had been friends with somebody for a decade
before they messaged me to say:

*Over the past year my life has changed from studying and education
to focusing on my career. Thank you so much
for all that you've done for me. Good luck with everything
and I wish you all the best in the future.*

We had been friends for so long and so badly that I had never considered what it might feel like to no longer have access to the information we knew and understood and loved? about each other. I thought he might want to die. He didn't.

The summer before I had been his plus one to his mother's second wedding. I had pressed play on the music system in the registrar's office. I had held her bouquet as we walked past the oolitic limestone, characteristic of the city of Bath, and I took candid photos of them both, content.

CREATING MORE DISTANCE BETWEEN YOU AND ANOTHER SPEAKER INDICATES UNCERTAINTY

Uncertainty feels comfortable and somewhat expected in games of Scrabble or Bananagrams. The only word I've encountered that begins with a double 'a' is aardvark. At the night safari in Singapore, I panicked and even now I'm unable to confirm whether I encountered a real aardvark in person and whether I had expected to or not.

You distance yourself from the truth.

I have panicked many times since then. Most recently, only moments ago when I couldn't sound the syllables out to sense in my braille assignment. I accepted the name given to my moments of panic but not until after I volunteered for a mood disorders experiment in which an MRI scan revealed my brain to be particularly symmetrical looking. I later found out this was a compliment in the radiology suite.
I welcomed the name of my new therapist until she asked why I wanted to work in a language that none of my friends or family spoke when she already knew that the answer was because none of my friends or family spoke it. She made me admit that anyway and annoyingly I felt better for it.

You distance yourself from the truth.

I don't want to lie to you but I don't want to tell you
the truth either.
I don't want to lie to you but I don't want to tell you
the truth either.
I don't want to lie to you but I don't want to tell you
the truth either.
I don't want to lie to you but I don't want to tell you
the truth either.
I don't want to lie to you but I don't want to tell you
the truth either.
I don't want to lie to you but I don't want to tell you
the truth either.
I don't want to lie to you but I don't want to tell you
the truth either.
I don't want to lie to you but I don't want to tell you
the truth either.
I don't want to lie to you but I don't want to tell you
the truth either.
I don't want to lie to you but I don't want to tell you
the truth either.
I don't want to lie to you but I don't want to tell you
the truth either.
I don't want to lie to you but I don't want to tell you
the truth either.
I don't want to lie to you but I don't want to tell you
the truth either.

You distance yourself from the truth.

The truth is that I never expect to fall in love.
The truth is that I've gotten very used to doing things by myself.
The truth is that I'll always be sat next to strangers on aeroplanes.
The truth is that I kissed somebody for the first time after a showing of *Priscilla Queen of the Desert* and went back to their flat to play on a VR headset because I'd never tried one before.
The truth is that I might have to get a dog one day.
The truth is that I'm worried a dog wouldn't love me either.
The truth is that the institution of marriage is discriminatory.
The truth is that I wouldn't feel beautiful in a white dress.
The truth is that a wedding would be really expensive anyway.
The truth is that I nearly have a housing deposit and mortgage affordability using just my own salary.
The truth is that I like sleeping in the middle of the bed.
The truth is that I like spending my evenings writing.
The truth is that I've already been to a power tools class.
The truth is that I can only fall asleep listening to Rain on Leaves or to Wind in Pines or to Celestial Sunbeams.
The truth is that I've always considered adoption.
The truth is that all or none of this is true.
The truth is that I'm kept awake at night thinking about Ewan McGregor, Nicole Kidman, and the recurring motif of *Moulin Rouge* where 'the greatest thing you'll ever learn is just to love and be loved in return'.

MY VOICE SOUNDS ENGLISH BUT LOOKS NORTHERN IRISH

I have spent a fourth of my life here. I know where I live
but I don't always know how to answer where I'm from.

In my first year of living here, I had a poem on the
Poetry Jukebox: a big blue tube that spouted poems
in C.S. Lewis Square. A journalist covering the launch
asked where I'm from. I've just moved to Belfast.
She asks again, Yes, but where in Belfast? and I say,
The city centre because I live in BT1 and I don't
understand that she's asking about cross-community relations.

Years later, I'm still living here but I'm a sports journalist
for a week at the Tokyo Paralympics. I don't know to sit
in the Press Tribunes and I've locked myself out of
the Olympic Information System. I am covering
the Wheelchair Fencing and am learning how to cover
the Wheelchair Fencing bout to bout. Everything is brilliant.

In the mixed zone, I interview my first athletes:
medallists from Team GB. Our accents
are not too far pitched from each other. I set up my voice
note app near the speaker and reread the questions
I've scribbled on the scoresheets. The PR representative
asks where I'm from and I say Northern Ireland because
I don't have a bed anywhere else. She asks again,
Yes, but which publication?

I delight in the jet lag and flinch at the amateur deluge
of not having pin badges or local goods to swap in expected

acts of global cooperation. Days later, I have witnessed joy and I have witnessed devastation.

Devastation is being one point away from your first gold medal match when your opponent finds the lamé just before you can. Devastation is ripping your mask off and letting it roll wherever it rolls. Devastation is throwing your foil over the side of your wheelchair and surrendering until your whole body accepts this moment of crisis and flops over the frame. Devastation is the volunteers rushing from the benches to sit you back up when you are more than capable of pulling yourself back up. Devastation is picking up your mask from the piste and putting it back on. Devastation is saluting your opponent, then the referee, as they call the point in your opposition's favour. Devastation is coming back out moments later to win a bronze medal but not yet being ready to speak about the possibility another touch held.

Devastation is writing a factual report of a 15-14 loss in a single sentence.

BEFORE I ARRIVE I ONLY LEARN BSL

Here, I use this form of *before* because it's combined with another action:

to arrive.

> There are visible and invisible
> borders, here, on this island:
> I shouldn't write about it.
> I have so much to learn.

> I have so much to learn
> and I don't do enough.
> People in a class in London
> don't recognize my handshapes
> even though I still remember
> how they pronounce their differences.
> I am tired of adjusting my accent.

> I have so much to learn
> and I don't do enough.
> The differences across the island
> extend beyond regional variations
> between signed and spoken languages.
> It takes six years before I meet
> quite casually an alphabet requiring
> higher dexterity of my thumb and vocabulary
> that I can only make guesswork at.

THERE IS MORE THAN ONE WAY TO TALK ABOUT THE YEAR AHEAD

It is my birthday so I am thinking about everything that has happened and everything that might be ahead.

I had asked for the thirteenth edition of a book all about pensions but was surprised by a bread machine that can also make jam. My friends come over and we drive to pick up sourdough pizzas. We negotiate how sad the film can be and I try to explain that yes, *Little Miss Sunshine* is sad in the ways that you wouldn't expect a birthday film to be but the sadness will pass and then there is just a lingering ache that is quite comforting and you'll be left either thinking of the lyrics of 'Super Freak' or the symphonic instrumentalism of 'Chicago' by Sufjan Stevens and which of those it is will be completely up to you.

Sometimes I trace a year across the back of my hand through the space between my index finger and thumb. Sometimes I flip my hand back over and look for the future held in the lines across my palm.

Even though we forget about the whoopie pie in the fridge and the candles are mentioned only in conversation, I don't know how to say that only the week before I remembered there was a box of candles in a drawer that had moved from house to house for five years because I couldn't bring myself to light the candles alone.

YOU CAN'T TELL ON PAPER BUT I'VE BRIEFLY SWAPPED TO A DIFFERENT LANGUAGE HERE

In a different language, I can live a different life.
I'm twenty-nine and I've been writing down my dreams for several years: for the business plans; for the poems.
I'm twenty-nine and renovating a listed but abandoned building with a generous grant from the government.
I'm twenty-nine and building a language school to host a language library with textbooks souvenired from a lifetime of non-working holidays. I'm twenty-nine and have worn a hard hat for weeks at a time and swatched sympathetic paint samples onto newly misted walls. I'm twenty-nine and have swept piles of miscellaneous rubble into bigger piles of
    miscellaneous rubble.
I'm twenty-nine and know to outsource the complicated works to the professionals, fairly paid for all the things they have learnt over time. I'm twenty-nine and I have created something new and beautiful.

IN MORE CASUAL MOMENTS OF HOPE ONLY ONE HAND IS NEEDED

Hopefully I can change lanes on the motorway in plenty of time. Hopefully I can slow dance to the radio. Hopefully I can sleep easily in this heat.

For the most hope, I cross both sets of fingers.

Hopefully I will visit my storage locker in Exeter and everything will be easily identifiable. Hopefully I'll be able to move out of the city soon. Hopefully I'll find a comfortable sofa on Facebook Marketplace. Hopefully I'll be good at DIY.

I prefer to ask the universe for the most hope.

Hopefully you understand that I'm writing these hopes and dreams on a weekday afternoon that I haven't forgotten about the climate crisis, that I'd like to write more ecopoetry, but I'm scared to read anything that mentions the moon.

I COULD'VE LISTED WHY I LOVE LANGUAGES RATHER THAN MOVE ON

THE SIGN FOR PEOPLE IN NORTHERN IRELAND IS MADE UP OF A WOMAN AND A MAN THE MORE I SIGN THIS THE MORE I WONDER HOW MUCH LONGER THE SIGN WILL BE IN CIRCULATION FOR

A south-east English regional variation of people, is close to how we in Northern Ireland sign electricity.

I remember this distinction by thinking of the spark people get when meeting their soulmates and of power ballads.

A suitable power ballad to listen to here to explain this phenomenon, if you have never experienced this spark of attraction, would be 'The Origin of Love' (from Hedwig and the Angry Inch). I bought my first car last year. I bought it because it was yellow. On a Monday, I thought I might like a car to ease the isolation of living on an island with no family on. On a Wednesday, I booked a viewing, applied for a zero per cent purchase credit card and on a Friday, got a tall male friend to drive to the industrial estate and check the car with me. On a Saturday, I paid for and drove the car home at twenty miles per hour.

In six months, I could count the number of people I've spoken to on one hand. The space I fill in the world feels smaller and smaller as the months pass and things don't seem to be getting better but the car is also mine now. In winter, I put on my coat. I take the blanket that I used to take on airplanes and a book. I lock myself in and sit under a streetlight for a while. I don't turn the car on, terrified of draining the battery, or wasting the petrol, so I play the radio through my phone and when 'I'd Do Anything for Love' comes on I sometimes sing along. The yellow glow of the bodywork and the breathless red of my cheeks is reflected in the street puddles, in the church windows, in the dark of the lonely evening.

THE FUTURE IS ALWAYS SLIGHTLY UNCOMFORTABLY AHEAD OF YOU

Nobody seems satisfied with what they have or where they are.

The next email could change your life. The next email will change your life. The next email could change your life. The next email will change your life. The next email could change your life. The next email will change your life. The next email could change your life. The next email will change your life. The next email could change your life. The next email will change your life. The next email could change your life. The next email will change your life. The next email could change your life. The next email will change your life. The next email could change your life. The next email will change your life. The next email could change your life. The next email will change your life. The next email could change your life. The next email will change your life. The next email could change your life. The next email will change your life. The next email could change your life. The next email will change your life.

**BUT I'M NERVOUS USUALLY I'M NERVOUS
I TAP MY HEART QUICKLY TO SHOW IT IS
BEATING QUICKER AND QUICKER**

Usually happens with regularity across the palm of the week.

This summer has been hotter than normal. The heat makes me nervous so I keep ice packs in the fridge. I'm an uneasy sleeper. A couple of times already this year, I've woken up hot and panicky. A mouse is living happily in my biscuit drawer. I've rolled out of bed and I'm away to the sofa downstairs. I carry the electric fan like a fleece blanket.

I can't lay down with my legs fully extended.
I'm crumpled over the unsupportive seat cushions.
The streetlights filter generously through the single glazing.
There will be a slug in the kitchen at this time of night.

It's possible that I'm having nightmares but I can't actually visualize anything in my head so I'm not sure I can have traditional nightmares or traditional dreams. The aphantasia also explains the face blindness and my callousness with unclose acquaintances.

**TRYING DOESN'T EXIST ENTIRELY
IN THE PRESENT YOU MUST BE MINDFUL
TO CARRY THE EFFORT INTO THE FUTURE**

Merlin is tangled in the thread of an unfinished upholstery project. In the same moment he realizes something is wrong, I lean over and to try to help him. He cowers and rips the thread away. He leaps up for comfort and rips my skin open.

Blood is oozing down both of my arms and staining my best pair of summer tights. I am quick with the antiseptic but find it difficult to watch the platelets clot. The bruises recolour themselves. To try, you must keep going.

I don't know when the last time I cut myself was. I nearly cry with the shock of it. To try, you must keep going. And going.

I go on a second date and drink a couple of cocktails. It is nearly Christmas. We go back to mine and sit on different sofas. We don't kiss. The next day they test positive and I sit at the kitchen table and try to remember if I opened the window.

I tell my housemate and she goes upstairs to pack a bag for the next ten days. I don't move from the table. Anticipation is my least favourite emotion. Heartbreak sounds like the slamming of a front door on an otherwise silent night.

To try, you must keep going. And going. And going.

It takes two years for me to realize
that when I say
which is like a metaphor
and my therapist says
psychological reason for
we are saying the same thing
in the language we know best.

INTERPRETERS CAN CHOOSE TO SPECIALIZE IN MANY AREAS OR NOT TO SPECIALIZE AT ALL

Two areas interpreters might consider themselves needed in are medicine and education. At the moment, I work in both.

On good days, I get to order the medical mannequins with interchangeable organs from *Limbs and Things*. On good days, I get to spend a morning walking around the university looking for an undelivered box of arms that I had arranged to be reskinned.

On other days, the box of arms in varying skin tones is found in the basement by somebody who wasn't expecting to open
 a box
of arms in varying skin tones and I regret to say I didn't get to hear their screams in person.

**NUMBERS GO OVER-MY-HEAD!
THIS STATEMENT ISN'T ACTUALLY TRUE
BUT IT WAS A GOOD OPPORTUNITY TO USE
A MULTI-CHANNEL SIGN**

A multi-channel sign must include the correct mouth pattern otherwise it is not a multi-channel sign. In exams, these are essential so the direction of the conversation will either be FANTASTIC! or I'll be GOBSMACKED!

Financial literacy is a growing interest of mine. I'd like to write a book about having four jobs and freelancing. I'm just waiting for the free time to do so.

I change the direction of conversation so that it is OVER-MY-HEAD!

To make some disposable income, I start matched betting. I didn't like supporting the horse racing industry and resent the gambling companies for obvious reasons of exploitation but I maintain that any appearance in my life will be limited.

It didn't matter which horse I picked as long as the odds for and against were comparable and I had enough liability in the exchange to cover the outcome.

It is both unfortunate (and planned) that in every exam so far I have had a MIND-BLANK!

I back a horse at 50/1 named Belfast Banter because I live in Belfast. The odds move before I can lay it and I say to myself I'll take another look in the morning. In the morning, I forget and the horse wins. It is a very fortunate mistake that funds a month of extravagance. I explain to my friend the next day that I bet on a horse which won so I'd like to buy the coffee. I know, I stop her, I'm not even trying to make it up. I swear.

**WHEN LEARNING TO SIGN IT IS BETTER PRACTICE
TO KEEP YOUR HANDS FREE
OF PENS PENCILS AND PAPER SO THAT YOU CAN
REPLICATE HANDSHAPES ACCURATELY FIRST TIME**

When I want to write, I go to the café above the high street bookshop that overlooks the travel agent. I have never used a travel agent. I am fascinated by the glossy brochures I catch bright and sticky colours from as the pages are flipped vicariously through in the waiting area. I'll often see people with a pencil behind their ear, or a pen between their teeth.

Not everybody remembers to bring a raincoat. A children's toy shop around the corner hasn't survived the pandemic. In a Faber-Castell display case, they are selling over eighty pencils in various, but not all sixteen, degrees of hardness. I arrive to find them pre-sharpened and know this is a good deal. What will I write with a decade's worth of pencils?

TELL ME IS A DIRECTIONAL VERB
THE FLOW OF INFORMATION MUST BE CLEAR

A friend of a friend who was at one point the fiancé of a friend tells me about a diagnosis that happened recently.

I research the diagnosis for a week before I call the GP. I have called at the wrong time of day. I call again at a different and still incorrect time of day. I call again even though I am tired now and so close to not calling again. The soonest appointment is in two weeks' time where I will be told a referral will likely take four years. I will be thirty then.

I wait for the doctor to tell me what I already know.

If I am going to tell other people, information extends from my lips into the empty crowd. The more people I tell, the longer the trail of information is left hanging in the air.

It is easier not to tell other people.

CAN YOU SEE BEHIND IN THE SEA PEOPLE ARE SWIMMING? IN THIS LANGUAGE SEA AND SEE ARE NOT HOMOPHONES

This was filmed before the resurgence of sea swimming and written before I moved closer to the sea. It was a shock to see people trusting themselves in the water on the early cusp of spring.

On a single-track road that runs too close to rock and lough, I meet two cars coming the other way and have to reverse around the corner screaming then back onto the empty concrete block I saw the swimmers edge themselves into the water from.

I leave the car and sit on the ledge, alone, my feet just shy of the lapping water, alone, the rough rock pushing grass and gravel into the back of my thighs. Alone. Two men swim around the island and at differing speed hold a conversation about the northwest anchorage. I have not been able to swim underwater for years. I do not trust my brain to remember to take a breath and hold it.
I try not to watch and instead envy the day-old croissants freshly buttered and set out on the fold up wooden table, its tablecloth bleached by the salt water.

CRUEL AND MEAT SHARE THE SAME HANDSHAPE AND MOVEMENT THE DIFFERENCE IS A MOUTH PATTERN AND CONTEXT

I went vegetarian at some point in the pandemic.
I ate some chicken I didn't like, and didn't eat any more.

I can't tell you when because in those months the days and
nights and mornings melted into each other and I never
opened my diary because to do so would mean to cross out
    another date
on the Harry Styles tour I had booked tickets for.

I had no more sense of adventure for food than I did
for the outside but there was no better time to eat
the things you wanted the most.

Look how many cheesecakes we've eaten!
I am delighted to have enjoyed so many of the same thing.
Later, we balance the splintered plastic recycling box
between us and relinquish the glass ramekins over to
    themselves.
A cacophony I refuse to subdue, I go to the shop and buy more.

I HAVE A SET OF FLASHCARDS FOR FEELINGS AND EMOTIONS

It is only after I disappoint myself, and other people, that I start writing again. If I am being honest, and I should be, I don't know
if I will ever be an interpreter. I don't know that I want to be anymore.

It is only after I watch somebody do something quite brilliant barefoot and with a window's view of Romania that I sign up for class again. I begin to tell if somebody is faking

their happiness by the height of their eyebrows.
One of my favourite people tells me they are engaged
and I haven't known happiness like it.

THERE IS A SUBTLE BUT SIGNIFICANT DIFFERENCE BETWEEN HAPPINESS AND JOY

The bigger the movement, the more likely I am to express joy.

I often keep my joy contained.

It has been days since I've spoken
to anyone else. Luckily, the days are short.

I bundle myself under the winter wool blanket on my bed.
I close my eyes. I listen to the voice notes my friends
have left me on speakerphone. Their voices fill the stillness
of the floorboards, the silence of the doorbell.

Sometimes I lose myself in the momentum of my own hands.
Joy turns into applause and I'm speaking another language again.

Acknowledgements

Previous publication credits: 'Target Demographic' was first published in *The Stinging Fly*. 'First Mistake' was first published in *Modern Poetry in Translation*. 'Let's Sign Science' was first published in *Prototype's Intertitles*. 'Let's Sign Minibeasts' was first published in *Fortnight Magazine*. 'Writing Audio Description at the Ulster Museum' was previously published in *Prototype's Intertitles* and UCD Press's *Hold Open the Door* and filmed for the Adrian Brinkerhoff Foundation. 'Tom Daley Dives for David Hockney / David Hockney Paints Tom Daley' was first published in *Gutter Magazine*. 'Sappho, who is doing you wrong?' was first published in *Modern Poetry in Translation*. 'The Lookout' was commissioned for Poetry as Commemoration by UCD, Poetry Ireland, the Department of Tourism, Culture, Arts, Gaeltacht, Sports and Media. A selection of work from [harbour doubts] has appeared in *Granta* and was awarded the Ivan Juritz Prize for Creative Experiment for Text.

    I am grateful to the Arts Council of Northern Ireland, Belfast City Council, Ards and North Down Council, Northern Bridge DTP, the Society of Authors and the Authors' Foundation for their various grants and bursaries in support of this work.

    The structure of [have] [have doubts] [harbour doubts] was inspired by the same phrase which appears in Yoko Tawada's *Portrait of a Tongue: An Experimental Translation* by Chantal Wright.

    Thank you to Laura Cassidy, Eimear Ryan, and Jessica Traynor for all their work and enthusiasm in bringing *Harbour Doubts* to bookshelves beyond my own.

Thank you to all of the poets who have read previous drafts of these poems. By sharing your thoughts and encouragement, you have made this work better.

Thank you to those of you who don't identify as poets but who have given their time and supported me anyway in this publication (and a vast array of other projects that I've worked on alongside this book). Thank you to all of my sign language teachers and to everybody that I've ever signed with. If you've ever wanted to learn sign language, please do try! You'll never regret learning to better communicate a part of yourself to others.

BANSHEE
PRESS

Banshee Press was founded by writers Laura Cassidy, Claire Hennessy and Eimear Ryan. Since 2015, *Banshee* literary journal has published twice a year. In 2021, Jessica Traynor joined Banshee Press as poetry editor.

The Banshee Press publishing imprint launched in 2019, publishing the very best in new fiction, poetry and memoir. Banshee Press authors include Dylan Brennan, Lucy Sweeney Byrne, Gustav Parker Hibbett, Claire-Lise Kieffer, Mary Morrissy, Deirdre Sullivan, Rosamund Taylor and David Toms.

WWW.BANSHEEPRESS.ORG